Autograph Celebrity COOKBOOK

Introduced and Compiled by Professor Richard Brown,
New York University

Foreword by Michael Lomonaco
Chef/Director, Windows on the World

A.J. Battifarano
Food Stylist

Lisa Sacco
Prop Stylist

Peter Johansky
Photographer

Doug Banquer
Designer

Autograph Celebrity COOKBOOK

Contents

Acknowledgements

We wish to thank the following for their contributions, without which this book would not have been possible:

A.J. Battifarano, Food Stylist

Elizabeth Beck, Cohn & Wolfe

Jennifer Bickman, Cohn & Wolfe

Professor Richard Brown, New York University

Gregory Chernin, Photography Assistant

Carole Coleman, Karlitz & Company

Simone Donahue-Chance, Meyer Corporation

Kristin Finio, DuPont Corporation

Sandra Rose Gluck, Food Editor

Barbara-Jo Howard, Cohn & Wolfe

Suzanne Howard, Meyer Corporation

Christa Kaiser, DuPont Corporation

Herb Karlitz, Karlitz & Company

Marcia Lerner, RR Donnelley & Sons Company

Amy Lord, Food Stylist

Mark Misilli, Meyer Corporation

Sonia Ortiz, RR Donnelley & Sons Company

Lisa Sacco, Prop Stylist

Norman Schoenfeld, Meyer Corporation

Sandi Schroeder, Schroeder Indexing Services

Ann Simonetti, Cohn & Wolfe

Sundberg & Associates

Introduction

I have been teaching the art of the motion picture at New York University for over twenty-five years. As part of my work, it has been my privilege to meet–and often get to know–many of today's most gifted film artists. Several of them have generously contributed favorite recipes to this book.

This project–and the task of assembling these recipes–set me to thinking about the intricate relationship between food and fame–between celebrated dishes and celebrated filmmakers. I realize that it gives us a special and unique pleasure to discover what our favorite stars enjoy at the dinner table. Here, after all, is a bit of intimacy which we can savor without ever being intrusive–or feeling that we are invading their privacy.

I have often thought that my friends and colleagues–the filmmakers and stars of this generation–have nurtured millions around the world with their splendid work and their memorable performances. Now, with this cookbook, they add a new dimension to the nurturing by graciously providing us a glimpse into their very personal tastes in the culinary arts.

Bon appetit!

Richard Brown

Richard Brown has been a professor at New York University since 1969. In appreciation for Professor Brown's compiling the celebrity recipes, DuPont has made a donation to support film education and, in particular, the Save Our Movies Fund, a project to restore and preserve film under the auspices of The Library of Congress.

Foreword

Great food is something that unites us all. Whether you are a movie star, athlete, TV sitcom actor, or someone like yourself, we all appreciate a wonderful meal and the steps that go into preparing one.

This book is a compilation of favorite recipes from some of the best-loved celebrities in America today. As you can see from their recipes, they really aren't so different from us–they like simple, imaginative, and easy to prepare dishes that everyone can enjoy. Our recipe "collaborators" deserve a lot of credit for their willingness to share their favorite personal recipes–it demonstrates that they, just like the rest of us, love food and appreciate good cooking.

At Windows on the World our menus read like a roadmap to the best American cooking around. Savory, sophisticated, aromatic, and enticing, the dishes we create and serve at our restaurant reflect "a new generation of American cooking." We believe our dishes have tradition, but are also current and alive–full of flavor and vitality just like the American spirit.

Our hope is that this book's celebrity recipes will inspire you to be creative in your kitchen–use fresh, locally grown, and natural ingredients as much as possible and don't be afraid to experiment or tweak the ingredients to assert your personality and to suit your tastes.

Keep the preparation and cooking time within reason to allow yourself as much time to spend with your guests as possible. Prepare and measure ingredients in advance or have each course ready to pop in the oven at the appropriate time. Use non-stick cookware like those with DuPont Autograph® non-stick coating to provide superior food "release" that won't sacrifice the integrity of the dish (recipes come out perfect without the concern of sticking), cut down on the clean-up time, and allow you to spend more time with your friends and family.

Enjoy!

Michael Lomonaco

Michael Lomonaco is Chef/Director of Windows on the World, host of "Michael's Place" on The Food Network and co-host of "Epicurious" on the Discovery Channel.

Alan Alda

Probably best known for his eleven-year role as Hawkeye Pierce in *M*A*S*H*, Alan also wrote, directed, and produced numerous episodes.

A true renaissance man, Alan has worked in virtually every area of show business. His first break was starring on Broadway in *The Owl and the Pussycat*. Film roles include *Manhattan Murder Mystery*, *Jake's Women*, *Betsy's Wedding*, *Crimes and Misdemeanors*, and *The Four Seasons*.

Alan's latest role was as a guest star for one season on the popular television series *ER*.

Pasta with Artichokes and Fava Beans

A stockpot fitted with the pasta insert is very handy–no need to use a colander, just toss the pasta with the artichoke sauce.

DIRECTIONS

■ In a large bowl, combine the water and lemon juice; set aside.

■ With a paring knife, remove the bottom of each artichoke stem, then trim off the dark outer layer. With your fingers, begin removing the dark outer leaves of the artichokes until the leaves are green at the top and light yellow at the bottom. Trim off the top green part of each artichoke. When very little green shows, cut off all the tips with a kitchen scissors. Quarter the artichokes and scrape out the choke. Cut each quarter in half again. As you clean each artichoke, transfer it to the bowl of lemon-water.

■ In a 4- or 5-quart sauté pan, heat the oil over medium heat. Add the garlic and cook 1 minute. Drain the artichokes and add to the pan; stir to coat. Cook, stirring, 5 minutes. Add the cold water, $\frac{1}{2}$ teaspoon of the salt, and the pepper and bring to a boil. Reduce the heat, cover, and simmer gently 15 minutes, adding more cold water if necessary.

■ Add the fava beans, cover, and cook until the artichokes and favas are tender, about 5 minutes longer. Add the parsley and remove the pan from the heat. Swirl in the butter until creamy.

■ Meanwhile, in an 8-quart stockpot of boiling salted water, fitted with the pasta insert, cook the pasta until "al dente." Drain the pasta and add it to the pan with the artichokes and favas; mix well. Remove the pan from the heat, add the cheese, and mix again. Serve immediately with a twist of black pepper on each serving.

Serves 4 to 6

Ingredients

- 6 cups cold water
- 2 tablespoons fresh lemon juice
- 4 large artichokes
- $\frac{1}{4}$ cup olive oil
- 3 cloves garlic, minced
- 1 cup cold water
- $\frac{3}{4}$ teaspoon salt
- $\frac{1}{2}$ teaspoon freshly ground black pepper
- 1 cup shelled fresh fava beans or peas
- $\frac{1}{4}$ cup chopped fresh Italian parsley
- 2 tablespoons cold unsalted butter, cut up
- 1 pound penne rigate or any ridged tubular pasta
- $\frac{1}{2}$ cup freshly grated Pecorino Romano cheese

Sautéed Shrimp with Basil and Cherry Tomatoes

Ingredients

2	tablespoons olive oil
1½	pounds large shrimp, shelled and deveined
3	cloves garlic, minced
1	pint cherry tomatoes, halved
⅓	cup finely chopped fresh basil
⅓	cup chicken broth or clam broth
½	teaspoon freshly grated orange zest
½	teaspoon salt

This simple preparation relies on the freshest ingredients–sweet cherry tomatoes, basil, and shrimp.

DIRECTIONS

■ In a 14-inch non-stick skillet, heat the oil over low heat. Add the shrimp and garlic and sauté until lightly colored, but not cooked through, about 1 minute.

■ Add the tomatoes, basil, broth, orange zest, and salt and cook, stirring frequently, until the shrimp are just cooked through and the tomatoes have started to collapse, about 2 minutes longer.

Serves 4

Adam Arkin

Widely known today as Dr. Aaron Shutt on the hit series *Chicago Hope*, Adam's first feature film appearance was in *The Monitors* in 1969.

Following in his father's footsteps (actor-director Alan Arkin), Adam has turned in many superb performances in films, including *A Slight Case of Murder*, *The Doctor*, *A Promise to Keep*, and *Under the Rainbow*.

Adam has played numerous roles on television, including the series *Happy Days* and *Barney Miller*. He has also starred in and directed episodes of *Northern Exposure* and *Chicago Hope*.

French Onion Soup

Long, slow cooking gives this soup its distinctive sweet, mellow flavor and deep rich color. For the best flavor, choose sweet Spanish, Vidalia, or Maui onions.

DIRECTIONS

■ In a 5-quart stockpot, heat the butter over medium-low heat. Add the onions, cover, and cook, stirring occasionally, 30 minutes. Uncover and cook until the onions are rich golden brown and very tender, 1¼ hours longer.

■ Add the sherry, raise the heat to high, and cook, uncovered, until the sherry has evaporated, about 3 minutes. Add the broth, water, thyme, salt, and pepper and bring to a boil. Reduce the heat, partially cover, and simmer until the broth is full-flavored, about 20 minutes.

■ Preheat the broiler with the rack 6 inches from the heat source. Toast the bread on the rack until golden brown, about 1 minute per side. Sprinkle the cheese on 1 side of the bread and broil, cheese side up, until the cheese has melted, about 30 seconds. Spoon the soup into 6 bowls, top each with 2 slices of the cheese bread, and serve.

Serves 6

Ingredients

2	tablespoons unsalted butter
4	pounds Spanish, Vidalia, or Maui onions, halved and thinly sliced
½	cup dry sherry
4½	cups canned chicken broth (or homemade if you have it)
3	cups water
¾	teaspoon dried thyme
½	teaspoon salt
½	teaspoon freshly ground black pepper
12	(½-inch-thick) slices Italian bread (3" x 2" each)
8	ounces shredded Gruyère cheese

Adam Arkin

Lentils du Puy with Roasted Carrots and Beets

Ingredients

5	tablespoons extra-virgin olive oil
3	small beets (12 ounces total), peeled and diced
1	large carrot (6 ounces), peeled and diced
4	shallots, peeled and halved
1½	(12 ounces) du Puy or other green lentils, picked over and rinsed
1¼	teaspoons salt
½	teaspoon freshly ground black pepper
2	sprigs fresh parsley
2	sprigs fresh thyme
4	cups boiling water
3	tablespoons sherry wine vinegar
¼	cup chopped fresh parsley

Du Puy lentils, small and dark green, are prized in France for their nutty flavor and firm yet tender texture. If you can't find them, substitute other green lentils.

DIRECTIONS

■ Preheat the oven to 400°F. In a 5-quart Dutch oven, combine 3 tablespoons of the oil, the beets, carrot, and shallots, stirring to coat the vegetables. Bake, uncovered, until the vegetables begin to color, about 30 minutes.

■ Stir in the lentils, salt, pepper, parsley, thyme, and water. Cover and bake until the lentils are tender and all the water has been absorbed, about 1 hour. Remove the parsley and thyme sprigs; discard. Stir in the vinegar, chopped parsley, and the remaining 2 tablespoons oil and serve.

Serves 6

Alan Arkin

A forty-year show business veteran, Alan made his mark in improvisation with the legendary Second City of Chicago.

His film-acting debut was in *The Russians Are Coming! The Russians Are Coming!* Two years later he played the sensitive deaf-mute hero in *The Heart Is a Lonely Hunter*.

Other film appearances include *The In-Laws*, *Jakob the Liar*, *Slums of Beverly Hills*, *Gattaca*, *Glengarry Glen Ross*, *The Rocketeer*, *Havana*, *Edward Scissorhands*, and *Catch-22*.

In recent years he has returned to his first love–Broadway.

Alan Arkin

Roquefort-Stuffed Burgers

Ingredients

1½   pounds ground sirloin

1   tablespoon Dijon mustard

2   teaspoons ketchup

½   teaspoon freshly ground
      black pepper

6   ounces Roquefort cheese

Shape the burgers with a tender hand and they'll remain juicy and light in texture. Using a non-stick grill pan allows you to grill at home indoors no matter what the weather.

DIRECTIONS

■ In a medium bowl, combine the sirloin, mustard, ketchup, and pepper. Divide the mixture into 4 equal portions. Divide the Roquefort into 4 portions. With your fingers, compress each portion of cheese into a ball. Shape 1 portion of the sirloin mixture around each Roquefort ball. Gently shape each into a 1-inch-thick pattie.

■ Heat a 12-inch non-stick grill pan over medium heat until hot. Add the burgers and cook 4 to 5 minutes per side for medium. Serve atop toasted buns, if you like.

Serves 4

Alan Arkin

Baked Beans

The non-stick surface of the Dutch oven makes clean-up a snap and the handle is oven-safe to 350°F.

DIRECTIONS

■ Preheat the oven to 250°F. In a Dutch oven or baking dish, stir together the beans, sugar, vinegar, chutney, maple syrup, garlic, chili powder, cloves, basil, salt, mustard powder, and thyme. Scatter the onion slices over the top and pour the coffee over them. Cover and bake 3 hours. Uncover and bake until the beans are richly flavored and the liquid is slightly thickened, about 2 hours longer. Serve with a salad, if you like.

Serves 6

Ingredients

2	cans (15 ounces each) kidney beans with their liquid
²/₃	cup packed brown sugar
½	cup cider vinegar
½	cup mango chutney, chopped
½	cup maple syrup
2	cloves garlic, peeled and crushed
2	tablespoons chili powder
4	whole cloves
1	teaspoon dried basil
½	teaspoon salt
½	teaspoon dried mustard powder
½	teaspoon dried thyme
2	large onions, thinly sliced
½	cup brewed coffee

Richard Belzer

Richard Belzer became a television superstar for his portrayal of Detective John Munch in *Homicide: Life on the Streets*.

Starting out as a stand-up comedian, Richard has built a reputation as a superb actor. His film and television roles include: *The Invaders, Hart to Hart, Lois and Clark, Mad Dog and Glory, The Wrong Guys, America, Night Shift, The X Files, The Larry Sanders Show, Mad About You*, and *Miami Vice*.

Currently, Richard has brought his talent and his character "Munch" to *Law & Order*.

Asparagus and Gruyère Strata

Perfect for brunch, the strata may be assembled the night before, then baked in the morning. If entertaining a larger crowd, double the recipe.

DIRECTIONS

■ In a 3-quart saucepan of boiling salted water, cook the asparagus 1 minute to blanch. Drain well; gently pat dry with paper towels.

■ Arrange the bread slices, slightly overlapping, in a 4-quart oven-safe sauteuse or baking dish. In a medium bowl, whisk together the eggs, milk, rosemary, salt, and pepper. Stir in the cheese. Scatter the asparagus over the bread and pour the milk mixture over the top. With a fork, prick several holes in each slice of bread (for better absorption of the milk mixture). Cover and refrigerate at least 30 minutes or up to overnight.

■ Preheat the oven to 325°F. Uncover and bake until the custard is set, the strata is puffed, and a knife inserted in the center comes out clean, about 40 minutes.

Serves 8

Ingredients

12 ounces asparagus, trimmed, peeled, and cut into 1-inch lengths

12 (1-inch-thick) slices firm, white, sandwich bread

10 large eggs

3   cups milk

½   teaspoon dried rosemary, crumbled

½   teaspoon salt

½   teaspoon freshly ground black pepper

6   ounces shredded Gruyère cheese

Richard Belzer

Artemis' Lamb Wrapped in Phyllo

Ingredients

Marinade
¼	cup plain yogurt
⅓	cup white wine
⅓	cup milk
¼	teaspoon fresh lemon juice
¼	teaspoon dried rosemary
¼	teaspoon dried mint
⅛	teaspoon salt
⅛	teaspoon cayenne
1	small clove garlic, peeled
1	teaspoon freshly grated Parmesan cheese
¼	cup chopped fresh tomatoes
2	tablespoons diced onion
2	tablespoons diced green pepper

Stuffing
½	cup freshly grated Parmesan cheese
¼	cup finely chopped fresh parsley
6	cloves garlic, minced
½	teaspoon salt
½	teaspoon freshly ground black pepper
4	(8-ounce) lamb steaks cut from leg

Wrapping
8	(12" x 17") sheets phyllo dough, halved crosswise
4	tablespoons olive oil
4	slices (1 ounce each) kasseri cheese
2	teaspoons unsalted butter

Niko, of Niko's Mediterranean Grill & Bistro in New York City, prepares this dish by special request for Richard. Double the recipe for a large dinner party.

DIRECTIONS

■ For the marinade: In a food processor or blender, combine the yogurt, wine, milk, lemon juice, rosemary, mint, salt, ground red pepper, garlic, Parmesan, tomatoes, onion, and green pepper and whirl until smooth. Transfer to a large bowl.

■ For the stuffing: In a small bowl, stir together the Parmesan, parsley, garlic, salt, and pepper. With a paring knife make shallow slits in the lamb. Rub the stuffing mixture all over the lamb and into the slits Add the lamb to the bowl of marinade, cover, and refrigerate 2 hours.

■ Preheat the oven to 350°F. Place 4 half-sheets of phyllo side by side on a work surface. Brush each with olive oil, top each with a second sheet, brush with olive oil, and repeat until each stack has 4 sheets.

■ With a slotted spatula, lift the lamb from the marinade. Place 1 lamb steak in the center of each stack. Top each with ½ slice of cheese. Top each slice of cheese with ½ teaspoon of the butter. Fold the sides in over the top and roll the remaining edges in to seal. Make several slits in the top to allow steam to escape.

■ Place the phyllo packets in a rectangular non-stick roasting pan. Brush each with olive oil; bake 20 minutes. Reduce the heat to 325°F and bake until golden brown and the lamb is cooked through, about 30 minutes longer.

Serves 4

Illeana Douglas

Associated with Martin Scorsese early in her career, Illeana provided the memorable scream in *Last Temptation of Christ*, played the mafioso wife in *Goodfellas*, and starred in *Cape Fear*.

Illeana's grandfather was the revered Melvyn Douglas, her grandmother the legendary Helen Gahagan Douglas.

She has starred in numerous independent films, including *Message in a Bottle* and *The Next Best Thing*, and played major roles on television, including *The Larry Sanders Show* and *Seinfeld*. Illeana began her directing career in 1993 with *The Perfect Woman*.

Potato-Crusted Red Snapper

Instant mashed potatoes and freshly grated Parmesan cheese give the fish its delicious crust.

DIRECTIONS

■ In a shallow plate, stir together the potatoes, Parmesan, parsley, and salt. In a separate bowl, stir together the egg and milk. Dip the fish first in the egg mixture, then in the potato mixture, pressing it in until the fish is well coated on both sides.

■ In a 12-inch skillet, heat the oil over medium heat. Add the fish and cook, turning it over as it colors, until golden brown and crusty, about 3 minutes per side. Serve with lemon wedges, if you like.

Serves 4

Ingredients

1   cup uncooked instant mashed potatoes

$1/2$ cup freshly grated Parmesan cheese

2   tablespoons chopped fresh parsley

$3/4$ teaspoon salt

1   large egg

1   tablespoon milk

4   (6- to 8-ounce) skinless, boneless red snapper fillets

2   tablespoons plus 2 teaspoons vegetable or olive oil

Lemon wedges, optional

Spring Vegetable Stew with Asparagus and Baby Peas

Ingredients

4	small, thin leeks (12 ounces total)
2	tablespoons olive oil
2	cloves garlic, slivered
8	ounces fresh shiitake mushrooms, stems trimmed and caps thickly sliced
1	pound small new potatoes, well scrubbed and quartered (cut in eighths if large)
³/₄	teaspoon salt
¹/₂	teaspoon rubbed sage
¹/₄	teaspoon freshly ground pepper
1¹/₂	cups water
8	ounces thin asparagus, trimmed and cut on diagonal into 1-inch lengths
1	cup fresh or frozen baby peas
2	tablespoons chopped fresh parsley

Serve this stew alongside a thick steak, pork chop, or fish fillet.

DIRECTIONS

■ Trim the leeks, discarding the tough green leaves. Cut the remainder in half lengthwise and then crosswise into 1-inch lengths. Place the leeks in a bowl of warm water; let the leeks sit until they are well washed. With your fingers, scoop the leeks out.

■ In a 3-quart covered saucepan, heat the oil over low heat. Add the garlic and cook, stirring frequently, 1 minute. Add the leeks, raise the heat to medium, and cook, stirring frequently, until crisp-tender, about 4 minutes. Add the mushrooms and cook until the mushrooms begin to wilt, about 3 minutes. Add the potatoes, salt, sage, pepper, and water and bring to a boil. Reduce the heat to low, cover, and simmer until the potatoes are tender, about 15 minutes. Uncover, add the asparagus and peas, and cook until the asparagus are tender, 3 to 4 minutes longer. Stir in the parsley and serve.

Serves 4

Richard Dreyfuss

Richard received an Academy Award in 1977 for his performance as Elliot Garfield in *The Goodbye Girl*. He was, at the time, the youngest actor so honored.

He is respected as a fiercely intelligent, thinking man's actor and is selective about the roles he takes. He has appeared in almost fifty films, including *The American President, Mr. Holland's Opus, Lost in Yonkers, Postcards From the Edge, Down and Out in Beverly Hills, Stand By Me,* and *Close Encounters of the Third Kind.*

Braised Chicken with Rosemary and Garlic

Wine, prosciutto, rosemary, and garlic give this dish its special flavor.

DIRECTIONS

■ In a 5-quart covered sauté pan, heat the oil over medium heat. Dredge the chicken in the flour, gently shaking off the excess. Sauté the chicken, half at a time, until golden brown, about 3 minutes per side. With a slotted spoon, transfer the chicken pieces to a platter; set aside.

■ Add the garlic, rosemary, and prosciutto to the pan and cook 1 minute. Add the white wine; cook 1 minute. Add the broth, salt, and pepper and bring to a boil. Return the chicken to the pan. Reduce the heat, cover, and simmer, turning the pieces over midway, until the chicken is cooked through, about 30 minutes.

■ Transfer the chicken to a large serving platter. Stir the parsley into the pan juices and spoon them over the chicken.

Serves 4

Ingredients

2	tablespoons olive oil
1	(3½-pound) chicken, skin removed and cut into 10 pieces
2	tablespoons all-purpose flour
4	cloves garlic, minced
2½	teaspoons finely chopped fresh rosemary
2	ounces prosciutto, finely chopped
⅓	cup dry white wine
1	cup chicken broth
¾	teaspoon salt
½	teaspoon freshly ground black pepper
2	tablespoons chopped fresh Italian parsley

Richard Dreyfuss

Triple Chocolate Pudding with White Chocolate Drizzle

DIRECTIONS

■ In a 2-quart non-stick saucepan, combine the milk, ¼ cup of the sugar, the cinnamon, orange zest, and salt and bring to a simmer over low heat. Remove from the heat, cover, and set aside 10 minutes to allow the flavor to develop. Remove and discard the orange zest.

■ In a small bowl, stir together the cocoa powder, cornstarch, and the remaining ¼ cup sugar until well combined. Return the milk mixture to the heat and bring to a simmer. Whisk about ½ cup of the hot milk mixture into the cocoa mixture. Whisk the cocoa mixture back into the milk and cook, stirring continuously, until the mixture comes to a boil. Continue to cook, stirring continuously, until the pudding thickens, about 1 minute. Remove the pan from the heat. Add the semisweet and milk chocolate, cover, and let stand until the chocolate has melted, about 5 minutes. Uncover and stir the mixture. Stir in the vanilla extract. Pour the pudding into 6 serving dishes. Cool to room temperature, then cover and refrigerate until set and well chilled, at least 2 hours

■ Place the white chocolate in a double-boiler insert or in a small bowl set over a pan of warm water; stir just until the chocolate melts. Drizzle the melted chocolate over the puddings. Chill 30 minutes longer and serve.

Serves 6

Ingredients

2½	cups whole milk
½	cup firmly packed dark brown sugar
½	teaspoon ground cinnamon
3	strips orange zest
⅛	teaspoon salt
3	tablespoons unsweetened cocoa powder
2	tablespoons cornstarch
4	ounces semisweet chocolate, coarsely chopped
2	ounces milk chocolate, coarsely chopped
1	teaspoon vanilla extract
2	ounces white chocolate

Olympia Dukakis

Olympia acted for decades before she was "discovered" in her Academy Award-winning role as wise mother Rose Castorini in *Moonstruck*.

She has played many superb character roles in numerous productions, including *Search for Tomorrow*, *The Neighborhood*, and *Rich Kids*.

Olympia's star status was confirmed in feature films and television, including *Better Living*, *The Pentagon Wars*, *Mr. Holland's Opus*, *Steel Magnolia*s, and *Working Girl*.

Olympia's husband is the brilliant character actor Louis Zorich (Paul Buchman's father on *Mad About You*, among other fine roles).

Greek Meatballs

Juicy and flavor-packed, these meatballs require no fat when using a non-stick pan. Olympia suggests making smaller meatballs for a buffet or for the kids.

DIRECTIONS

■ In a large bowl, combine the beef, veal, lamb, egg, milk, onion, mustard, tamari, ½ teaspoon of the oregano, the salt, garlic powder, vinegar, if using, and bread crumbs. With your hands, gently mix the ingredients until combined. Shape into 36 walnut-size meatballs.

■ Heat a 12-inch skillet over medium heat. Add half the meatballs and sprinkle them with ¼ teaspoon of the remaining oregano and 2 tablespoons of the parsley. Cook, gently turning the meatballs over as they brown, 5 to 7 minutes. Transfer to a platter and repeat with the remaining meatballs, oregano, and 2 tablespoons parsley. Transfer the last batch to the platter with the other meatballs, sprinkle with the remaining ¼ cup parsley, and serve.

Makes 36 large meatballs

Ingredients

½	pound ground beef
½	pound ground veal
½	pound ground lamb
1	large egg
¼	cup milk
1	large onion, coarsely chopped
2	teaspoons Dijon mustard
1	teaspoon tamari or soy sauce
1	teaspoon dried oregano
¾	teaspoon salt
½	teaspoon garlic powder
2	drops red wine vinegar, optional
⅓	cup plain dry bread crumbs, cornmeal, or wheat germ
½	cup chopped fresh parsley

Olympia Dukakis

Pan-Cooked Cornish Game Hens with Lemon and Hot Pepper

The non-stick double-burner pan can accommodate both Cornish hens at once and cook them quickly and evenly with very little fuss because it utilizes both burners.

DIRECTIONS

■ In a large bowl, combine the rosemary, salt, crushed red pepper, and black pepper. Add the hens and, with your hands, rub the seasoning mixture into the hens. Add the olive oil and lemon slices and toss well to combine. Cover and refrigerate at least 4 hours or up to overnight.

■ Heat a 10″x 18″ non-stick double-burner pan over medium heat. Lift the Cornish hens from the marinade and place, skin side down, in the pan; discard the marinade. Cook, turning the hens several times, until they are cooked through and browned, 30 to 40 minutes. Serve with lemon wedges, if you like.

Serves 4

Ingredients

- $3/4$ teaspoon dried rosemary, crumbled
- $3/4$ teaspoon salt
- $1/2$ teaspoon crushed red pepper flakes
- $1/4$ teaspoon freshly ground black pepper
- 2 ($1^{1}/_{4}$-pound) Cornish game hens, split lengthwise
- 3 tablespoons olive oil
- 1 lemon, thinly sliced

Lemon wedges, optional

Griffin Dunne

One of the brightest of the new generation of stars, Griffin is a multi-talented film figure who has acted in almost thirty films since 1975.

A talented producer, he first produced *Head Over Heels* in 1979, and has successfully produced six other features, including *Once Around, White Palace, Baby It's You, Running on Empty,* and *After Hours.*

Griffin's memorable acting roles include *Search and Destroy, I Like It Like That, Quiz Show, Johnny Dangerously,* and *An American Werewolf in London.*

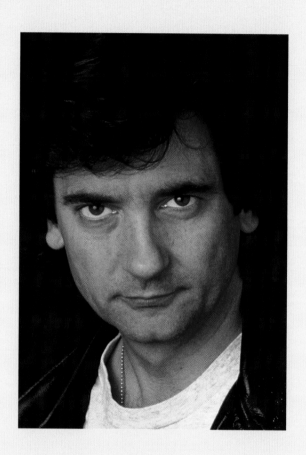

Plum Upside-Down Cake

Ingredients

3	tablespoons plus 1 stick unsalted butter, at room temperature
1/4	cup firmly packed light brown sugar
2	pounds (about 8) black plums, halved, pitted, and halved again
1½	cups all-purpose flour
2	teaspoons baking powder
1/4	teaspoon baking soda
1/4	teaspoon salt
1	cup granulated sugar
2	large eggs, separated
1	teaspoon freshly grated lemon zest
1/2	cup buttermilk
1	teaspoon vanilla extract
1/4	teaspoon cream of tartar

Butter and brown sugar are melted together in an oven-safe sauté pan and topped with cut plums. The batter is poured over the fruit mixture and then it's baked in the cookware. After cooling briefly, the cake is slipped out of the pan onto a waiting cake plate.

DIRECTIONS

■ Preheat the oven to 350°F. In an oven-safe 10-inch sauté pan or metal baking dish, over low heat, melt 3 tablespoons of the butter with the brown sugar. Arrange the plums, skin side down, in a circular fashion, atop the butter-sugar mixture; set aside.

■ In a medium bowl, stir together the flour, baking powder, baking soda, and salt. In the large bowl of an electric mixer, beat the granulated sugar with the remaining stick of butter until light and fluffy. Beat in the egg yolks, one at a time, until well blended. Beat in the lemon zest. Combine the buttermilk and vanilla extract. On low speed, alternately beat in the flour mixture and buttermilk, beginning and ending with the flour. In a separate bowl, beat the egg whites and the cream of tartar until foamy. Continue beating until the egg whites form soft peaks. Gently fold the beaten whites into the batter.

■ Spoon the batter over the plums, smoothing the top. Bake until the top is golden brown and a cake tester inserted toward the outside of the sauté pan comes out clean, about 40 minutes. Let the cake cool 10 minutes in the pan, then run a spatula around the edge to release the cake and invert it onto a cake plate. Serve warm or chilled.

Serves 8 to 10

Griffin Dunne

Chicken Teriyaki

DIRECTIONS

■ In a plastic zip-tight bag, combine the soy sauce, sugar, sesame oil, ginger, and 2 of the scallions. Add the chicken breasts; seal the bag, pressing out the air; and refrigerate, turning the bag occasionally, at least 1 hour or up to overnight.

■ Brush a 9 ½-inch non-stick square grill pan with vegetable oil. Heat the pan over medium heat. Lift the chicken from the marinade and place in the pan; discard the marinade. Grill 5 minutes, then turn and grill until the chicken is cooked through and richly browned, 5 to 7 minutes longer. Transfer the chicken to a large platter.

■ Meanwhile, in a dry 8-inch skillet, over medium heat, toast the sesame seeds, shaking the pan frequently, until the seeds are golden brown, 1 to 2 minutes. Sprinkle the sesame seeds and the remaining scallion over the chicken and serve.

Serves 4

Ingredients

1/3	cup soy sauce
2	tablespoons light brown sugar
1	tablespoon Asian sesame oil
3/4	teaspoon ground ginger
3	scallions, thinly sliced
4	large skinless, boneless chicken breast halves (about 1½ pounds)
2	teaspoons vegetable oil
1	tablespoon sesame seeds

Hector Elizondo

Hector has undertaken a broad variety of roles with a stunning range. Most familiar to fans now as *Chicago Hope*'s Dr. Phillip Walters, Hector is a favorite of director Garry Marshall. He's appeared in Marshall's *Runaway Bride*, *The Other Sister*, and *Pretty Woman*, to name just a few.

Hector's other work includes outstanding performances in *Safe House*, *Beverly Hills Cop III*, *The Burden of Proof*, *The Fan*, *Taking Care of Business*, *The Flamingo Kid*, and *American Gigolo*.

Black Bean Chili

There's no need to soak the black beans overnight, but if you like, cook the beans early in the day (or the day before), then proceed with the recipe.

DIRECTIONS

■ For the beans: In a 5-quart Dutch oven or stockpot, bring the beans and water to a boil over high heat. Reduce the heat, cover, and simmer 45 minutes, adding more water if necessary to cover the beans. Strain, reserving 2 cups cooking liquid, adding water if necessary to make 2 cups.

■ Rinse and dry the Dutch oven, add the oil, and heat over medium heat. Sauté the pork in 2 batches until golden brown, about 5 minutes per batch. With a slotted spoon, transfer the pork to a bowl; set aside.

■ Add the onion and garlic to the pan and cook, stirring frequently, until the onion is tender, about 7 minutes. Stir in the chili powder, cumin, coriander, and oregano and cook 2 minutes longer.

■ Stir in the tomatoes, salt, pork, beans, and reserved cooking liquid and bring to a boil. Reduce the heat, cover, and simmer until the pork and beans are tender, about 1 hour.

Serves 4

Ingredients

1	cup dried black beans, picked over and rinsed
4	cups water
2	tablespoons olive oil
1¼	pounds boneless pork shoulder, cut into ½-inch chunks
1	large onion, finely chopped
3	cloves garlic, minced
2	teaspoons medium-hot chili powder
1½	teaspoons ground cumin
1	teaspoon ground coriander
1	teaspoon dried oregano
1	cup canned crushed tomatoes, with their juice
¾	teaspoon salt

Hector Elizondo

Easy Baked-Tomato Pasta

Try this recipe at the height of summer, when tomatoes are at their best. If you're cooking a smaller batch of pasta, use a 4-quart pasta pot with insert.

DIRECTIONS

■ Preheat the oven to 400°F. Line the bottom of an oven-safe 10-inch covered sauteuse or baking dish with half the sliced tomatoes. Spoon the anchovies, their oil, and ½ teaspoon of the salt over the tomatoes. Top with the remaining tomatoes, remaining ½ teaspoon salt, black pepper, and crushed red pepper flakes. Pour the olive oil over the top, cover, and bake until the tomatoes are soft and saucy, about 20 minutes.

■ Meanwhile, in an 8-quart stockpot of boiling salted water with the pasta insert in place, cook the pasta until "al dente"; drain. Transfer the pasta to a large bowl. Pour the tomatoes and their liquid over the pasta, add the Parmesan and parsley, and toss to combine. Pass additional Parmesan and black pepper, if you like.

Serves 6

Ingredients

2	pounds ripe plum tomatoes (preferably Romas), cored and thickly sliced
1	(2-ounce) can flat anchovies in olive oil
1	teaspoon salt
¾	teaspoon freshly ground black pepper
¼	teaspoon crushed red pepper flakes, or to taste
½	cup extra-virgin olive oil
1	pound spaghetti or linguine
¾	cup freshly grated Parmesan cheese
½	cup chopped fresh parsley

Andy Garcia

Andy is a focused and caring actor who has built a formidable career. His carefully chosen roles span a broad variety of films.

His films include *Swing Vote*, *Just the Ticket*, *Desperate Measures*, *Hoodlum*, *Death in Granada*, *Night Falls on Manhattan*, *Steal Big, Steal Little*, *When a Man Loves a Woman*, *The Godfather Part III*, *The Untouchables*, and *Stand and Deliver*.

Born in Cuba, Andy emigrated to Miami and attended Florida International University in the 1970s, with a theater major.

Cuban Black Beans and Rice

Start soaking the beans early in the day, then cook them slowly in a non-stick soup pot. Sofrito, used in Latin American cooking, is a mixture of pork, green pepper, onion, garlic, and herbs that is sautéed in olive oil and used to flavor soups, beans, and stews.

DIRECTIONS

■ For the beans: In a 5-quart stockpot, combine the beans, water, green pepper, and onion. Let stand at room temperature for 3 hours or up to overnight.

■ Place the pot over high heat and bring to a boil. Reduce the heat, cover, and simmer until the beans are tender, 45 minutes to 1 hour, adding more water if necessary to cover the beans. Strain, reserving 3 cups cooking liquid, adding water if necessary to make 3 cups. Discard the pepper and onion.

■ Rinse and dry the pot. Prepare the sofrito: Cook the pork over medium heat until lightly browned. With a slotted spoon, transfer the pork to a bowl. Add the oil to the pot and heat over medium-low heat. Add the onion, green pepper, and garlic and cook, stirring occasionally, until the onion is tender, about 10 minutes.

■ Stir in the salt, pepper, oregano, bay leaf, sherry, beans, and reserved cooking liquid and bring to a boil. Stir in the rice and return to a boil. Reduce the heat, cover, and simmer gently until the rice is tender, about 20 minutes. Let stand 5 minutes; remove the bay leaf and discard. Makes 12 cups.

Serves about 8

Ingredients

Beans

1 ¼	cups (8 ounces) dried black beans, picked over and rinsed
5	cups cold water
1	large green pepper, trimmed, seeded, and quartered
1	large onion, peeled and quartered

Sofrito

8	ounces lean pork, diced
1	tablespoon olive oil
1	large onion, diced
1	large green pepper, trimmed, seeded, and diced
6	cloves garlic, minced
1½	teaspoons salt
½	teaspoon freshly ground black pepper
1	teaspoon dried oregano
1	bay leaf
3	tablespoons dry sherry
1	pound (2 cups) extra-long-grain rice, rinsed

Andy Garcia

Sautéed Scallops and Spring Vegetables

Ingredients

3	tablespoons olive oil
2	small leeks, white and tender green parts, well washed and thinly sliced
2	cloves garlic, minced
2	teaspoons finely chopped, peeled fresh ginger
1	red pepper, trimmed, seeded, and julienned
8	ounces sugar snap peas, strings removed
½	cup chicken broth or clam broth
½	teaspoon salt
1½	pounds sea scallops, rinsed in cold water and patted dry
2	tablespoons all-purpose flour
1	tablespoon cold unsalted butter, cut up
2	tablespoons snipped fresh chives

You may substitute small bay scallops for the sea scallops; decrease the cooking time accordingly.

DIRECTIONS

■ In a 10-inch covered sauté pan, heat 1 tablespoon of the oil over medium heat. Add the leeks, garlic, and ginger and cook, stirring frequently, until the leeks are tender, about 7 minutes. Add the red pepper and sugar snap peas and cook until the vegetables are crisp-tender, about 3 minutes. Add the broth and salt and bring to a boil; remove from the heat.

■ Meanwhile, in a separate 14-inch non-stick skillet, heat the remaining 2 tablespoons of oil over medium-high heat. Dredge the scallops in the flour, shaking off the excess, and sauté, turning the scallops over as they color, until golden brown and cooked through, about 2 minutes. Add the scallops to the vegetable mixture and swirl to combine. Remove the pan from the heat and swirl in the butter until it has melted. Add the chives and serve.

Serves 4

Janeane Garofalo

Janeane has carved out a unique career in the entertainment industry. Starting on *The Larry Sanders Show* in 1992 (as Paula, the talent booker), she has distinguished herself as an actress, sketch comedian, and stand-up comic.

Janeane has appeared in such hit series as *Home Improvement*, *Seinfeld*, and *Mad About You*, and has turned in excellent performances in independent films such as *200 Cigarettes*, *Can't Stop Dancing*, *McClintock's Peach*, *The Minus Man*, and *Reality Bites*.

Spinach and Ricotta–Stuffed Lasagna Rolls

Ingredients

16	lasagna noodles (1 pound)
2	tablespoons olive oil
1	large onion, finely chopped
4	cloves garlic, minced
1½	cups ricotta cheese
½	cup freshly grated Parmesan cheese
1¼	teaspoons salt
½	teaspoon freshly ground black pepper
1	large egg
2	(28-ounce) cans crushed plum tomatoes, with their juice
1½	teaspoons freshly grated orange zest
⅛	teaspoon cayenne
2	(10-ounce) packages frozen leaf spinach, thawed and squeezed dry

An easy alternative to lasagna. If you prefer, substitute part-skim for the whole-milk ricotta. The rectangular roasting pan is attractive enough to go from oven to table.

DIRECTIONS

■ In an 8-quart stockpot of boiling salted water, cook the lasagna noodles until "al dente"; drain. Transfer the noodles to a large bowl of cold water to prevent sticking.

■ Meanwhile, in a 10-inch skillet, heat 1 tablespoon of the oil over medium heat. Add the onion and 3 cloves of the garlic and cook, stirring frequently, until the onion is tender and lightly golden, about 7 minutes. Transfer to a large bowl. Stir in the ricotta, Parmesan, 1 teaspoon of the salt, the black pepper, and the egg until well combined.

■ In the same skillet, heat the remaining tablespoon of oil over low heat. Add the remaining garlic and cook 1 minute. Add the tomatoes and their juice, the orange zest, cayenne, and the remaining ¼ teaspoon salt and bring to a boil. Reduce the heat and simmer until the flavors develop, about 5 minutes.

■ Preheat the oven to 350°F. Drain the noodles and pat dry. Arrange a row of spinach leaves down the center of each lasagna noodle. Spread equal portions of the ricotta mixture over the spinach. Starting at 1 short end, roll the noodles up. Place, seam side down, in a non-stick rectangular roasting pan. Spoon the tomato mixture over the noodles, cover with aluminum foil, and bake until the noodles and sauce are piping hot, about 25 minutes.

Serves 8

Janeane Garofalo

Dried-Cherry Scones

If you like, prepare the dry ingredients along with the butter the night before, then assemble and bake the scones just before serving.

DIRECTIONS

■ Preheat the oven to 375°F. In a large bowl, stir together the flour, 2 tablespoons of the sugar, the baking powder, baking soda, and salt. With a pastry blender or 2 knives used scissors fashion, cut in the butter until the mixture resembles coarse meal. Add the cherries; toss to combine.

■ In a small bowl, stir together the buttermilk and egg yolk. Pour the buttermilk mixture over the flour mixture and toss with a fork until a soft dough forms. Transfer the dough to a lightly floured work surface and knead 6 or 7 times, or until a ball is formed. Flatten the ball into an 8-inch round; cut into 8 wedges but do not separate the wedges. Transfer to a 10-inch skillet.

■ In a small bowl, beat the egg white and water until the white is just broken up. Brush over the round and sprinkle the top with the remaining teaspoon of sugar. Bake until set and lightly golden, 18 to 20 minutes. Cool 5 minutes in the pan, then separate into wedges and serve either warm or at room temperature.

Serves 8

Ingredients

1 1/2	cups all-purpose flour
2	tablespoons plus 1 teaspoon sugar
2	teaspoons baking powder
1/4	teaspoon baking soda
1/4	teaspoon salt
6	tablespoons cold unsalted butter, cut up
3/4	cup dried cherries
1/2	cup buttermilk
1	large egg, separated
1	teaspoon water

Scott Glenn

Scott is closely associated with the archetypical American cowboy, as he embodies the strength and decency of the Old West. Fans might be interested to learn that he is a New Yorker and has studied with some of America's finest acting teachers.

Scott has also scored many of his finest acting triumphs live on the New York stage. His many productions include *Fortune and Men's Eyes* and *Collision Course*.

Scott's star appearances on television and film include *Firestorm*, *Carla's Song*, *The Hunt for Red October*, *The Player*, and *Apocalypse Now*.

Shrimp Marinara

If you like, you may cook the marinara sauce in advance, label, and freeze it. Once the sauce is made, dinner is done in no time.

DIRECTIONS

■ In a 3-quart saucepan, heat 1 tablespoon of the oil over medium heat. Add the onion and cook, stirring frequently, until tender, about 5 minutes. Add the tomatoes and their juice, the salt, sugar, and pepper and bring to a boil. Reduce the heat and simmer, uncovered, until the sauce is thick, about 15 minutes. Set aside.

■ In a 12-inch skillet, heat the remaining 2 tablespoons of oil over medium-high heat. Sauté the shrimp until just cooked through, about 3 minutes. Return the sauce in the pan to a simmer. Transfer the heated sauce to a bowl, add the shrimp, and toss to combine. Sprinkle with the basil and serve.

Serves 4

Ingredients

3	tablespoons olive oil
1	medium onion, finely chopped
1½	pounds ripe plum tomatoes, cored, peeled, and coarsely chopped (or 1½ cups canned tomatoes, coarsely chopped, with their juice)
½	teaspoon salt
½	teaspoon sugar
¼	teaspoon freshly ground black pepper
1½	pounds large shrimp, shelled and deveined
2	tablespoons chopped fresh basil

Scott Glenn

Yukon Gold Potato Gratin

DIRECTIONS

■ Preheat the oven to 400°F. In a 3-quart saucepan, melt the butter over low heat. Whisk in the flour until well combined. Gradually whisk in the milk until blended. Stir in the garlic, salt, and pepper and cook, stirring frequently, until the sauce is smooth and thick, about 5 minutes. Strain through a fine-meshed sieve; discard the garlic.

■ Arrange a layer of potatoes over the bottom of the oven-safe pan or baking dish, overlapping the slices slightly. Spoon ¼ of the milk mixture over the potatoes. Top with another layer of potatoes, half of the remaining milk mixture, a third layer of potatoes, half of the remaining milk mixture, and the remaining potatoes. Spoon the remaining milk mixture over the potatoes.

■ Cover and bake 45 minutes. Sprinkle the cheese over the top and bake until the top is browned and the potatoes are piping hot and tender, about 20 minutes longer. Let stand 10 minutes before serving.

Serves 6

Ingredients

3	tablespoons unsalted butter
¼	cup all-purpose flour
4	cups milk
4	cloves garlic, peeled and crushed
1¼	teaspoons salt
¾	teaspoon freshly ground black pepper
2¾	pounds Yukon Gold potatoes, peeled and cut into ¼-inch-thick slices
¾	cup freshly grated Parmesan cheese

Tony Goldwyn

Tony is the grandson of Samuel Goldwyn, scion of a family that has represented cinematic "royalty" for almost a century. A talented actor, Tony honed his skills at The London Academy of Dramatic Art before working in New York theater, where he has performed in numerous productions.

Tony has made guest appearances on television shows, including *St. Elsewhere* and *L.A. Law* and has played leading roles in feature films, including *The Lesser Evil*, *The Pelican Brief*, and *Ghost*. Tony was also the voice of Tarzan in Disney's 1999 *Tarzan*.

Tony Goldwyn

Pork Tenderloin Steaks with Spicy Tomato Sauce

Ingredients

1	large pork tenderloin (about 1½ pounds)
¾	teaspoon salt
½	teaspoon freshly ground black pepper
2	tablespoons olive oil
4	cloves garlic, minced
1½	cups canned tomatoes, chopped, with their juice
2	tablespoons red wine vinegar
1	tablespoon Dijon mustard
2	teaspoons capers, rinsed and drained
¼	teaspoon cayenne
2	tablespoons chopped fresh parsley

Mustard, capers, and cayenne give this sauce its kick. Pork tenderloin, a lean cut, cooks up juicy and tender with very little oil in this non-stick skillet.

DIRECTIONS

■ Cut the pork tenderloin crosswise into 8 slices. Sprinkle the pork with ½ teaspoon of the salt and the pepper. In an 11-inch stir-fry or 12-inch skillet, heat the oil over medium-high heat and sauté the pork until cooked through, about 4 minutes per side. Transfer to a large platter.

■ Reduce the heat to low, add the garlic, and cook, stirring frequently, until the garlic is tender, about 2 minutes. Add the tomatoes, vinegar, mustard, capers, cayenne, and the remaining ¼ teaspoon salt. Cook, stirring occasionally, until the sauce is slightly reduced and flavorful, about 5 minutes longer. Stir in the parsley, spoon the sauce over the pork, and serve.

Serves 4

Tony Goldwyn

Lime-Chicken Pasta Salad

DIRECTIONS

■ In a large, plastic, zip-tight bag, combine ¼ cup of the olive oil, 4 tablespoons of the lime juice, ½ teaspoon of the black pepper, ¼ teaspoon of the salt, and the cayenne. Add the chicken and seal the bag, pressing out the air. Refrigerate at least 1 hour or up to 2 hours.

■ Meanwhile, in a large bowl, whisk together the vinegar, mustard, sugar, the remaining ½ teaspoon pepper, the remaining ¼ teaspoon salt, the remaining 2 tablespoons lime juice, and the remaining ½ cup olive oil. Add the onion, red and yellow peppers, cucumber, carrot, tomato, celery, and artichoke hearts and toss to combine.

■ Heat a 12-inch round stovetop grill pan over medium-high heat. With tongs, lift the chicken from the marinade; discard the marinade. Grill the chicken until cooked through, about 5 minutes per side. Cool to room temperature and thinly slice crosswise. Add to the bowl of vegetables and toss to combine.

■ Meanwhile, in a large pot of boiling salted water, cook the penne according to package directions; drain well. Add the pasta and the cheese to the chicken and toss to combine.

Serves 8

Ingredients

³/₄	cup olive oil
6	tablespoons fresh lime juice
1	teaspoon freshly ground black pepper
½	teaspoon salt
¼	teaspoon cayenne
4	large skinless, boneless chicken breast halves (about 1½ pounds)
2	tablespoons balsamic vinegar
1	teaspoon Dijon mustard
½	teaspoon sugar
1	Spanish onion, finely chopped
1	red pepper, trimmed, seeded, and thinly sliced
1	yellow pepper, trimmed, seeded, and thinly sliced
1	cucumber, peeled, halved lengthwise, seeded, and thinly sliced
1	large carrot, peeled and chopped
1	large tomato, cored, seeded, and coarsely chopped
1	stalk celery, coarsely chopped
1	(8-ounce) can artichoke hearts packed in water, drained
1	pound penne pasta
½	cup freshly grated Parmesan cheese

James Earl Jones

James Earl has led one of the most remarkable and inspiring careers in show business and has established a reputation as one of the country's most distinguished actors on stage and screen.

His voice is without question the best known in America. It became part of our collective consciousness in the first *Star Wars* over two decades ago, when he created the voice of Darth Vadar.

In 1999, James Earl completed his 100th feature film. His work includes *Primary Colors, Patriot Games, Field of Dreams, King Lear,* and *The Great White Hope.*

Chilean Sea Bass

Ingredients

3	tablespoons unsalted butter
10	Maui, Vidalia, or Spanish onions (5 pounds), halved and thinly sliced (15 cups)
12	Italian plum tomatoes, peeled, seeded, and coarsely chopped (or 4½ cups canned tomatoes, chopped, with their juice)
5	shallots, peeled and halved
3	cloves garlic, peeled and halved
3	fresh basil leaves, chopped
1	tablespoon extra-virgin olive oil
1	teaspoon salt
½	teaspoon ground white pepper
12	(2" x 2½") Chilean sea bass fillets (2½ to 3 pounds total)

Creamy Chilean sea bass stands up to this flavorful onion sauce. If you can't find Chilean sea bass, substitute black cod or cod.

DIRECTIONS

■ In a 5-quart sauteuse or baking dish, melt the butter over low heat. Add the onions and cook, stirring frequently, until they are rich golden brown, about 1½ hours.

■ Transfer the onions to a food processor. Add the tomatoes, shallots, garlic, and basil and puree until no lumps remain. Wipe the pan out and add the olive oil. Add the onion puree and cook over low heat, stirring occasionally, until the sauce is flavorful and no longer raw tasting, about 30 minutes.

■ Preheat the oven to 425°F. Place the bass in a small rectangular roasting pan, sprinkle them with the salt and pepper, and spoon the onion puree over the top. Bake until the fish is just cooked through, about 10 minutes. Divide the sauce evenly among 6 dinner plates and top each with 2 fish fillets.

Serves 6

James Earl Jones

Stir-Fried Minestrone

The 14-inch stir-fry has enough room to hold all the vegetables and a heavy enough surface to prevent sticking or burning. Here, minestrone soup is turned into a colorful stir-fry.

DIRECTIONS

▪ In a 14-inch stir-fry, heat the oil over medium heat. Add the bacon and cook until lightly crisped, about 4 minutes. With a slotted spoon, transfer the bacon to a paper-towel-lined plate to drain; set aside.

▪ Add the onion and garlic to the pan and cook, stir-frying, until the onion is lightly browned, about 5 minutes. Add the carrots, potato, zucchini, and green beans and stir-fry until the potato is crisp-tender, about 5 minutes. Add the cabbage and stir-fry until the cabbage is tender, about 4 minutes. Add the tomatoes and their juice, the cannellini beans, basil, salt, and bacon. Raise the heat to high and cook 2 minutes.

▪ In a small bowl, stir together the broth and cornstarch. Pour the mixture into the pan and cook, stirring continuously, 1 minute. Transfer to 4 serving plates, sprinkle with Parmesan, and serve.

Serves 4

Ingredients

2	tablespoons olive oil
2	slices bacon (about 2 ounces), coarsely chopped
1	large onion, cut into 1/2-inch chunks
2	cloves garlic, minced
2	carrots, peeled, halved lengthwise, and cut crosswise into 1/2-inch lengths
1	Idaho potato, peeled and cut into 1/4-inch chunks
1	medium zucchini, halved lengthwise and cut crosswise into 1/2-inch-thick slices
6	ounces green beans, trimmed and halved lengthwise
3	cups chopped fresh cabbage or kale
1	cup canned tomatoes, chopped or crushed, with their juice
1	cup cooked cannellini beans, rinsed and drained
1/4	cup chopped fresh basil
3/4	teaspoon salt
3/4	cup chicken broth
1	teaspoon cornstarch
1/3	cup freshly grated Parmesan cheese

Billie Jean King

As one of the twentieth century's most respected women, Billie Jean King has long been a champion for social change and equality. King created new inroads for women in and out of sports during her legendary career and she continues to make her mark today.

One of the most illustrious and celebrated tennis players in history, King is recognized for spearheading the women's movement in tennis and for her life-long struggle for equality in women's tennis. King empowered women and educated men when she defeated Bobby Riggs in one of the greatest moments in sports history, the Battle of the Sexes in 1973.

Crosscourt Cabbage Salad

Ingredients

1	(5-ounce) package slivered almonds
1	(5-ounce) package hulled sunflower seeds
¾	cup olive oil
½	cup sugar
½	cup balsamic vinegar
2	tablespoons soy sauce
1	medium head cabbage, shredded (about 8 cups)

DIRECTIONS

■ In a 2-quart saucepan, over medium heat, toast the almonds and sunflower seeds, stirring constantly to prevent burning, 2 to 3 minutes. Set aside to cool.

■ In a jar or bottle with a tightly fitting lid, combine the oil, sugar, vinegar, and soy sauce; shake well. Place the cabbage in a large bowl and sprinkle with the toasted nuts and seeds. Just before serving, pour the dressing over the cabbage and toss until evenly coated.

Serves 6

Swoosie Kurtz

A respected Broadway actress, Swoosie has worked in a broad variety of media, gaining millions of fans for her role as Alexandra Reed on the popular television series *Sisters*.

Swoosie won an Obie in 1999 for her virtuoso performance in the two lead roles of the play *The Mineola Twins*. She won a Tony for her performance in *House of Blue Leaves*.

She has starred in numerous films and TV productions, including *Cruel Intentions*, *Reality Bites*, *Bright Lights, Big City*, and *Dangerous Liaisons*.

Creamy Basmati Rice Pudding with Pistachios

While it may seem like overkill to use a 4-quart saucepot for the rice, it will boil over in a smaller pan. The non-stick finish keeps the rice from sticking.

DIRECTIONS

■ In a 4-quart covered non-stick saucepot, stir together the milk, sugar, orange zest, vanilla bean, cardamom, salt, and cloves. Stir in the rice and bring to a boil over medium heat. Reduce the heat, cover, and simmer gently until the rice is very tender and creamy, 35 minutes. Cool to room temperature.

■ Transfer the cooled rice to a bowl. Stir in the pistachios and raisins, cover, and refrigerate until well chilled.

Serves 4

Ingredients

1	quart whole milk
½	cup sugar
6	(2″ x ½″) strips orange zest
½	vanilla bean, split lengthwise
½	teaspoon ground cardamom
⅛	teaspoon salt
⅛	teaspoon ground cloves
¾	cup basmati rice, rinsed and drained
¾	cup shelled pistachios, toasted
½	cup golden raisins

Swoosie Kurtz

Wild Rice à la Swoosie

Ingredients

8	ounces (1¼ cups) wild rice
5	strips bacon (4 ounces), cut into thin strips
1	large onion, diced
5	stalks celery, trimmed and diced
4	ounces mushrooms, trimmed and thinly sliced
2	tablespoons all-purpose flour
2¼	cups whole milk
¾	teaspoon salt

DIRECTIONS

■ In a medium bowl, combine the rice with enough cold water to cover by 2 inches. Let stand at room temperature at least 2 hours or up to overnight. Drain.

■ In a 2-quart saucepan of boiling salted water, cook the rice 20 minutes; drain. Transfer the rice to a colander and rinse under hot running water. Place the colander over a pan of simmering water, cover, and steam until the rice is tender, about 15 minutes.

■ Preheat the oven to 325°F. Meanwhile, in a 5-quart covered Dutch oven, cook the bacon over medium-high heat until lightly crisped. With a slotted spoon, transfer the bacon to a paper-towel-lined plate; set aside.

■ Remove all but 2 tablespoons of the bacon drippings from the pan. Add the onion and celery and cook, stirring occasionally, until the onion is tender, about 10 minutes. Add the mushrooms to the pan and cook, stirring frequently, until the mushrooms are tender, about 5 minutes. Add the flour and cook 2 minutes, stirring continuously, until well coated. Stir in the milk and salt and cook, stirring continuously, until lightly thickened and smooth. Gently stir in the rice. Bake, uncovered, until piping hot, about 10 minutes.

Serves 6

Robert Loggia

One of the most recognized and respected faces in the performing arts, Robert started as a youngster four decades ago with a small part in the film *Somebody Up There Likes Me*.

He has done guest appearances on fifty television shows, ranging from *Playhouse 90* in the 1950s, to *Little House on the Prairie* and *Quincy*.

Robert's brilliant work has appeared in a stunning 100 movies over his career, including *Bonano: A Godfather's Story*, *Innocent Blood*, *Prizzi's Honor*, *Scarface*, and *Casino*.

Veal Cutlets Milanese

If you prefer, you can substitute chicken cutlets for the veal.

DIRECTIONS

■ In a shallow bowl or pie plate, lightly beat the eggs with the milk. In a separate bowl or on a sheet of waxed paper, combine the Parmesan cheese, bread crumbs, oregano, and salt.

■ Dip the veal first in the egg mixture, then in the Parmesan mixture, until well coated. (You can do this up to 4 hours ahead of cooking, then place the coated chicken on a plate, cover loosely, and refrigerate.)

■ In a 10-inch skillet, heat 1 tablespoon of the oil over medium heat until hot but not smoking. Add 2 slices of veal and sauté until golden brown and just cooked through, about 1½ minutes per side. With tongs or a kitchen fork, transfer the cooked veal to a platter. Repeat, using 1 tablespoon of oil for every 2 slices of veal. Divide evenly among 4 dinner plates and serve with lemon wedges, if you like.

Serves 4

Ingredients

2	large eggs
1	tablespoon milk or cream
1	cup (2 ounces) freshly grated Parmesan cheese
¾	cup plain dry bread crumbs
2	teaspoons dried oregano
½	teaspoon salt
8	(¼-inch-thick) slices (1½ pounds) veal scaloppine
4	tablespoons olive oil
	Lemon wedges, optional

Robert Loggia

Herb-Rubbed Chicken Breast with Tropical Salsa

Ingredients

2	teaspoons chopped fresh oregano
1	teaspoon chopped fresh thyme
1	teaspoon coarse (kosher) salt
1/2	teaspoon sugar
1/8	teaspoon ground allspice
1/8	teaspoon cayenne
4	skinless, boneless chicken breast halves (about 1 1/2 pounds)
1	large mango, peeled, pitted, and cut into 1/2-inch chunks
1	small banana, cut into 1/2-inch chunks
1	small red pepper, trimmed, seeded, and finely chopped
2	scallions, thinly sliced
1/4	cup fresh lime juice
2	tablespoons honey

This tropical salsa also goes well with grilled pork or fish. The non-stick grill pan gives the chicken a hot-off-the-barbecue finish and there's no messy cleanup.

DIRECTIONS

■ In a small bowl, stir together the oregano, thyme, salt, sugar, allspice, and cayenne. Rub the mixture into the chicken, cover, and refrigerate 30 minutes.

■ Meanwhile, in a large bowl, stir together the mango, banana, red pepper, scallions, lime juice, and honey. Cover and refrigerate.

■ Heat a 9 1/2-inch grill pan over medium heat. Grill the chicken until cooked through, turning the chicken several times as it cooks, about 5 minutes per side. Transfer the chicken to 4 dinner plates, top each serving with a spoonful of the salsa, and serve.

Serves 4

Michael Lomonaco

Michael's restaurant experience reads like a "Who's Who" of culinary institutions. Prior to joining Windows on the World in 1997 as Chef/Director, Michael served as Executive Chef at New York's vaunted '21' for eight years, before which he sharpened his skills and lent his considerable talents to the legendary Maxwell Plum's and the world-famous Le Cirque.

His work has earned him accolades from not only restaurant patrons, but revered restaurant critics as well. His fan base grew exponentially when he assumed the post as the talented and charismatic host of The Food Network's highly rated *Michael's Place* and as co-host of Discovery Channel's *Epicurious* food show. Michael is also a published writer and author of *The '21' Cookbook*.

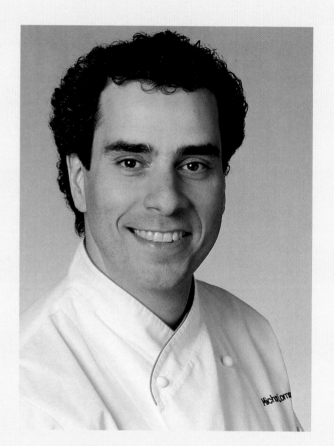

Pan-Roasted Halibut with Spring Vegetables

DIRECTIONS

■ In a medium saucepan of boiling water, cook the asparagus tips and fava beans 30 seconds to blanch; drain. Run under cold water to stop the cooking; drain again.

■ Season the halibut with the salt and pepper. In a 10-inch open French skillet, heat the oil over medium-high heat. Add the fish, flesh side down, and sauté 4 minutes. Turn and sauté, skin side down, 4 minutes.

■ Add the blanched asparagus tips and fava beans to the pan and cook 2 minutes. Add the wine and cook 1 minute. Remove the pan from the heat, add the butter and tarragon, and swirl until creamy.

Serves 4

Ingredients

1	cup pencil-thin asparagus tips
1/2	cup shelled fresh fava beans
4	(6-ounce) halibut fillets
1/2	teaspoon salt
1/4	teaspoon freshly ground black pepper
2	tablespoons olive oil
1/4	cup white wine
1	tablespoon unsalted butter
3	tablespoons chopped fresh tarragon leaves

Michael Lomonaco

Raspberry French Toast

Ingredients

1   cup high-quality seedless raspberry jam

1   (1-pound) loaf day-old brioche bread or other rich, slightly sweet bread, cut into 16 thin slices

6   eggs

1½   cups milk

¼   cup orange liqueur

1   tablespoon vanilla extract

¼   teaspoon salt

4   tablespoons unsalted butter

Confectioners' sugar

2   (½-pint) baskets fresh raspberries, picked over

Warm maple syrup

Sour cream

DIRECTIONS

■ Preheat the oven to 250°F. Spread a thin layer of jam on 1 side of each slice of bread and fold in half to form sandwiches. In a large bowl, whisk together the eggs, milk, orange liqueur, vanilla extract, and salt. Dip the sandwiches into the egg mixture and soak briefly.

■ In a 12-inch non-stick skillet, heat 1 tablespoon of the butter over medium heat. Working in batches, sauté the sandwiches until golden brown, about 2 minutes per side. Repeat with the remaining sandwiches, adding butter as needed.

■ Transfer the sandwiches to a large heatproof platter and keep warm in the oven until all the sandwiches have been cooked. Garnish with the fresh raspberries and dust with confectioners' sugar. Serve with maple syrup and sour cream.

Serves 8

Michael Lomonaco

The Classic Omelet

Omelets cook in no time, so for best results, cook one a time. The non-stick skillet is a perfect substitute for an omelet pan—the eggs don't stick and the omelet slides right out of the pan.

DIRECTIONS

■ In a medium bowl, whisk together the eggs, water, salt, and pepper just until the yolks and whites are blended.

■ Heat a 7-inch skillet over high heat. Add the butter and swirl it around until it coats the bottom of the pan and the foam subsides. Quickly pour in the egg mixture and stir, pulling the set eggs in from the outer edge to the center, until the eggs are just set.

■ With a rubber spatula, start rolling the omelet onto itself by tipping the pan forward. Roll the omelet out of pan onto a serving plate, seam side down.

Serves 1

■ For filled omelets: Add cooked vegetables, cheese, or meats to the center of the omelet just before you begin to roll the finished omelet onto the plate. Always heat fillings separately and cut the meat and cheese thinly enough to be thoroughly heated by the heat in the center of the omelet.

■ Suggested fillings:
Sautéed mushrooms and goat cheese
Fresh herbs: thyme, chives, tarragon, parsley
Sautéed spinach
Cheddar cheese and jalapeño pepper
Cooked bacon or country ham
Ratatouille

Ingredients

3	large eggs
1	tablespoon water
1/4	teaspoon salt
1/4	teaspoon freshly ground white pepper
1	tablespoon butter or vegetable or olive oil

Penelope Ann Miller

In the mid-1980s, Penelope Ann made a stunning Broadway debut as Daisy in Neil Simon's *Biloxi Blues*. She reprised the role in 1988, when Mike Nichols brought it to the screen. She has since starred in *The Freshman*, *Kindergarten Cop*, *Chaplin*, and *Carlito's Way*.

Penelope Ann's other performances include leading roles in *All The Fine Lines*, *Chapter Zero*, *Killing Moon*, and *The Last Don*. She has also made several notable guest appearances on television in *St. Elsewhere*, *Miami Vice*, *The Facts of Life*, and *Family Ties*.

Lobster Bisque

Ingredients

3	tablespoons plus 1¼ teaspoons salt
1	(2½-pound) live Maine lobster
3	tablespoons unsalted butter
½	cup plus 3 tablespoons minced shallots
4	cloves garlic, minced
⅓	cup cognac
3	cups dry white wine
3	tablespoons tomato paste
1	tablespoon chopped fresh parsley
2	teaspoons dried tarragon
½	teaspoon dried thyme
Pinch of crushed red pepper flakes	
2	small bay leaves or 1 large
3	tablespoons all-purpose flour
2½	cups milk
¾	cup heavy cream
2	large egg yolks

If you can't find a 2½-pound lobster, substitute two 1½-pounders. Either way, the large stockpot can accommodate the lobster(s).

DIRECTIONS

■ In a 12-quart stockpot, bring 2 gallons (32 cups) of water to a boil. Add 3 tablespoons of the salt and return to a boil. Add the lobster and cook until the lobster is bright red and cooked through, about 12 minutes. Set aside 4 cups of the cooking water. When cool enough to handle, remove the lobster meat from the shell and finely dice; discard the shell.

■ In a 3-quart saucepan, melt 1 tablespoon of the butter over medium heat. Add ½ cup of the shallots and the garlic and cook, stirring frequently, until the shallots are tender, about 5 minutes. Add the cognac, raise the heat to medium-high, and cook until the cognac has evaporated, about 2 minutes. Stir in the wine, tomato paste, parsley, tarragon, thyme, crushed red pepper flakes, bay leaves, and the reserved 4 cups lobster cooking liquid and bring to a boil. Reduce the heat and simmer, uncovered, 30 minutes; strain.

■ In a separate 3-quart saucepan, melt the remaining 2 tablespoons butter over medium heat. Add the remaining 3 tablespoons shallots and cook, stirring frequently, 2 minutes. Whisk in the flour and cook, whisking continuously, until blended, about 1 minute. Gradually whisk in the wine mixture and cook until well blended and lightly thickened, about 5 minutes. Whisk in the milk, cream, and the remaining 1¼ teaspoons salt and bring to a simmer.

■ In a small bowl, whisk the egg yolks until blended. Whisking continuously, add ½ cup of the hot liquid, then whisk the yolk mixture back into the pan. Stir in the lobster meat and cook, stirring continuously, until well blended and slightly thickened, 3 to 4 minutes. Makes 10 cups.

Serves 8

Enchilada Casserole

Prepare this dish for a crowd. Salsa verde comes in varying degrees of heat so make this as mild or as hot as you like. Manchego cheese has a rich, nutty flavor. If you can't find Manchego substitute Monterey Jack, Fontina, or Gruyère.

DIRECTIONS

■ Preheat the oven to 375°F. In a 3-quart saucepan heat the oil over low heat. Add the red pepper and garlic and cook until the pepper has softened, about 3 minutes. Stir in the chili powder; cook 1 minute. Whisk in the flour until well combined. Gradually whisk in the milk. Cook, stirring continuously, until the sauce is slightly thickened, about 5 minutes. Remove from the heat and stir in 1 cup of the salsa verde, ¾ cup of the cheese, and the salt.

■ Spoon the remaining cup of salsa verde over 1 side of each tortilla and sprinkle with the chicken, tomato, cilantro, and remaining ¾ cup of cheese. Roll up the tortillas and place, seam side down, in a large rectangular roasting pan. Spoon the milk mixture over the tortillas and bake until piping hot, about 30 minutes.

Serves 8 to 12

Ingredients

3	tablespoons olive oil
1	red pepper, trimmed, seeded, and finely chopped
2	cloves garlic, minced
2	teaspoons chili powder
¼	cup all-purpose flour
2½	cups milk
2	cups jarred salsa verde
1½	cups shredded Manchego cheese
½	teaspoon salt
16	(7-inch) flour tortillas
12	ounces (about 3 cups) cooked chicken, shredded
1	large ripe tomato, cored and coarsely chopped
⅓	cup chopped fresh cilantro

Jerry Orbach

To millions of Americans, the name Jerry Orbach is synonymous with the tough, cynical detective Lennie Brisco on *Law & Order*. Jerry began his celebrated career on the stage playing the lead character El Guyo in the beautiful and haunting production of *The Fantastiks*, the longest running show in history.

His notable guest appearances on TV include *Homicide: Life on the Street*, *Murder She Wrote*, *The Golden Girls*, *Who's the Boss*, and *Kojak*. His feature films include *Chinese Coffee*, *Straight Talk*, *Mr. Saturday Night*, *Last Exit to Brooklyn*, *The Flamingo Kid*, *Crimes and Misdemeanors*, *Dirty Dancing*, and *Prince of the City*.

Chicken with Artichokes, Mushrooms, and White Wine

DIRECTIONS

■ In a bowl, combine the flour, ¼ teaspoon of the salt, and the pepper. Dredge the chicken in the flour mixture, shaking off the excess.

■ In a 10-inch skillet or sauté pan, heat the oil over medium heat. Sauté the chicken until golden brown, about 4 minutes per side. With a slotted spoon or kitchen fork, transfer the chicken to a platter.

■ Add the mushrooms to the skillet and cook, stirring frequently, until golden, about 4 minutes. Add the artichokes; stir to coat. Add the wine, sage, and remaining ½ teaspoon salt and bring to a boil. Return the chicken to the skillet. Reduce the heat, cover, and simmer until the chicken is cooked through and tender, about 30 minutes.

Serves 4

Ingredients

2	tablespoons all-purpose flour
¾	teaspoon salt
¼	teaspoon freshly ground black pepper
6	chicken thighs (1½ pounds), skin removed
1	tablespoon olive oil
4	ounces button mushrooms, trimmed and thinly sliced
1	(9-ounce) bag frozen artichoke hearts, thawed
1	cup white wine
½	teaspoon dried sage, crumbled

Jerry Orbach

Pan-Fried Steak with Balsamic Sauce

Ingredients

1	teaspoon ground cumin
1	teaspoon ground coriander
3/4	teaspoon salt
1/2	teaspoon freshly ground black pepper
4	(1-inch-thick) boneless sirloin steaks (about 2 pounds)
1	tablespoon olive oil
1	small red onion, finely chopped
1	clove garlic, minced
1	teaspoon finely chopped fresh rosemary
1/3	cup balsamic vinegar
1	teaspoon brown sugar
1	tablespoon cold unsalted butter, cut up

A small amount of brown sugar added to the sauce enriches the full, rich flavor of the aged balsamic vinegar used in this dish.

DIRECTIONS

■ In a small bowl, stir together the cumin, coriander, 1/2 teaspoon of the salt, and the pepper. Rub the mixture over the steaks.

■ In a 12-inch skillet or sauté pan, heat the oil over medium-high heat. Add the steaks and cook 3 to 4 minutes per side for medium-rare. Transfer the steaks to a large platter.

■ Add the onion and garlic to the pan and cook, stirring frequently, until the onion is lightly browned, about 3 minutes. Add the rosemary; stir to combine. Add the vinegar, sugar, and the remaining 1/4 teaspoon salt and bring to a boil. Cook until slightly reduced, about 2 minutes. Remove from the heat and swirl in the butter. Spoon the sauce over the steaks and serve.

Serves 4

John Sayles

John is credited by many with starting the movie industry's "independent" category. Though widely known as a director and writer, John has also done a good deal of acting, particularly (but not exclusively) in his own films.

He has also edited most of his own productions. His dazzling filmography includes *Alligators*, *Limbo*, *Lone Star*, *Passion Fish*, and *Baby, It's You*.

The unique brand of courage and creativity that John has brought to his film work won him the coveted MacArthur Citation (the legendary "genius" award).

Cajun Steak

If you prefer, use your favorite Cajun spice rub to season the steaks. A grill pan may be used in place of the skillet.

DIRECTIONS

■ In a small bowl, stir together the chili powder, thyme, oregano, onion powder, garlic powder, salt, pepper, sugar, and cayenne. Rub the mixture into both sides of the steaks.

■ In a 12-inch skillet or sauté pan, heat the oil over medium-high heat. Sauté the steaks 3 minutes per side for medium-rare or longer if you desire.

Serves 4

Ingredients

2	teaspoons chili powder
1½	teaspoons dried thyme, crumbled
1	teaspoon dried oregano, crumbled
¾	teaspoon onion powder
½	teaspoon garlic powder
½	teaspoon salt
½	teaspoon freshly ground black pepper
½	teaspoon sugar
¼	teaspoon cayenne
4	(1-inch-thick) rib-eye steaks (about 2 pounds)
1	tablespoon olive oil

Fajitas Chicanas

Ingredients

1	pound skinless, boneless chicken breast
8	teaspoons olive oil
³/₄	teaspoon salt
¹/₂	teaspoon freshly ground black pepper
1	red or green pepper, trimmed, seeded, and cut into thin strips
2	tablespoons plus 2 teaspoons soy sauce
1	large onion, peeled and cut into thick rounds
8	ounces mushrooms, trimmed and thinly sliced
8	(8-inch) flour tortillas, warmed
2	cups cooked black beans
2	cups cooked white rice

If you prefer, substitute 1 pound of skirt steak or 1 pound of shelled and deveined shrimp for the chicken breast.

DIRECTIONS

■ In a medium bowl, toss the chicken with the oil, salt, and pepper. Cover and refrigerate at least 1 hour or up to overnight.

■ Pour 2 teaspoons of the oil from the chicken into a 10-inch skillet over medium-high heat. Add the red pepper and 2 teaspoons of the soy sauce and cook until crisp-tender, about 5 minutes. Transfer to a bowl. Pour 2 teaspoons of the remaining oil into the skillet, add the onion and 2 teaspoons of the soy sauce, and sauté until crisp-tender, about 5 minutes. Transfer to the bowl with the pepper. Add 2 more teaspoons of the oil from the chicken and 2 teaspoons of the remaining soy sauce to the pan. Add the mushrooms and sauté until tender, about 5 minutes. Transfer to the bowl with the other vegetables.

■ Add the chicken with the remaining 2 teaspoons of oil to the pan. Sprinkle with the remaining 2 teaspoons soy sauce and sauté the chicken until golden brown and cooked through, about 5 minutes per side. With tongs, transfer the chicken to a platter and set aside to cool slightly.

■ When the chicken is cool enough to handle, starting at 1 long side, cut thin slices. Toss the chicken with the vegetables. Spoon the chicken and vegetables into the flour tortillas. Serve with the beans and rice.

Serves 4

Paul Sorvino &
Mira Sorvino

A gifted Broadway actor, Paul also lists writing, directing, and producing to his show business credits, along with superb tenor and chef.

On television, he has starred in *Law & Order* and had guest roles on *Star Trek* and *Murder She Wrote*. In film, Paul has starred in *Prince of Central Park*, *Bulworth*, *Houdini*, *Dick Tracy*, *Goodfellas*, and *Cry Uncle!*

With all his talents, Paul will say that his two greatest loves are the opera and his children. His daughter, Mira, won an Oscar for her role in *Mighty Aphrodite*.

A magna cum laude Harvard graduate, Mira's first role was in the television movie *Swans Crossing* in 1992. Since then she has turned in exceptional performances in *Quiz Show*, *Barcelona*, *Jake's Women*, *Norma Jean and Marilyn*, and *Joan of Arc, The Virgin Warrior.*

Rigatoni Bolognese

Start the pasta sauce early in the day, as it requires long, slow cooking to extract all of its delicate flavor.

DIRECTIONS

■ In a 4- to 5-quart Dutch oven or stockpot, heat the oil and butter over low heat. Add the onion and cook, stirring frequently, until tender, about 7 minutes. Add the carrot and celery and cook, stirring frequently, until tender, about 4 minutes.

■ Add the beef to the pan and cook just until no longer pink but not browned, about 3 minutes. Add the wine, raise the heat to medium-high, and cook, stirring frequently, until the wine has evaporated, about 7 minutes.

■ Lower the heat to medium-low, add the milk, and cook, stirring frequently, until the milk has been absorbed by the meat, about 10 minutes. Add the tomatoes and their juice and the salt. Cook, stirring frequently, until the sauce is thick and creamy, about 2 hours.

■ In an 8-quart saucepot of boiling water cook the rigatoni until "al dente"; drain. Toss the pasta with the hot sauce and pass the Parmesan separately.

Serves 4

Ingredients

1	tablespoon olive oil
1	tablespoon unsalted butter
1	small onion, finely chopped
1	small carrot, peeled and finely chopped
1/2	stalk celery, finely chopped
3/4	pound ground chuck
1	cup dry white wine
3/4	cup whole milk
2	cups canned tomatoes, chopped or crushed, with their juice
3/4	teaspoon salt
12	ounces rigatoni
1/2	cup freshly grated Parmesan cheese

**Paul Sorvino
& Mira Sorvino**

Chicken Breasts Stuffed with Black Forest Ham

Serve this elegant dish with a side of herbed couscous or rice and a green vegetable. Chicken breasts cooked in the pan remain moist and juicy.

DIRECTIONS

■ Place the chicken breast halves between 2 layers of plastic wrap or waxed paper and with a meat mallet or the flat side of a heavy pan, pound the chicken to a 1/4-inch thickness. (Alternately, have your butcher do this for you.) Sprinkle both sides of the chicken with salt and pepper. Place the ham so that it covers 1 side of each chicken breast half. Top each with some cheese and 2 sage leaves. Roll up the chicken from 1 short end. Secure with toothpicks.

■ In a 10-inch covered sauté pan, heat the oil over medium heat. Dredge the chicken in flour, shaking off the excess, and sauté, turning the chicken occasionally, until golden brown, about 5 minutes. Add the broth, lemon zest, and lemon juice to the pan and bring to a boil. Reduce the heat, cover, and simmer, turning the chicken occasionally, until cooked through, 10 to 15 minutes. Transfer the chicken to 4 plates and remove and discard the toothpicks.

■ Raise the heat to high and cook the broth 1 minute longer. Add the parsley and butter, remove the pan from the heat, and swirl just until the butter is melted. Spoon the sauce over the chicken and serve.

Serves 4

Ingredients

4	skinless, boneless chicken breast halves (about 1¼ pounds)
1/4	teaspoon salt
1/4	teaspoon freshly ground black pepper
4	ounces thinly sliced Black Forest ham
3	ounces shredded Gruyère cheese
8	fresh sage leaves
2	tablespoons olive oil
3	tablespoons all-purpose flour
3/4	cup chicken broth
1	teaspoon freshly grated lemon zest
2	tablespoons fresh lemon juice
3	tablespoons chopped fresh Italian parsley
1	tablespoon cold unsalted butter, cut up

Ben Stiller

This brilliant young actor and comedian has come by his talent with the best genes available in the business thanks to his mother, Anne Meara, and his father, Jerry Stiller.

A writer, producer, and director, Ben directed two episodes of *The Ben Stiller Show* as well as *The Cable Guy*, and *Reality Bites*.

His work includes outstanding performances in *There's Something About Mary*, *Fresh Horses*, *Empire of the Sun*, and *The Suburbans*.

Sweet Ricotta Pancakes

The double-burner pan allows you to cook a big batch of these luscious pancakes and to sit and enjoy them along with your guests.

DIRECTIONS

■ Spoon the ricotta into a strainer set over a bowl to catch drips. Let drain 1 hour.

■ In a large bowl, stir together the drained ricotta, the flour, 3 tablespoons of the sugar, the eggs, butter, vanilla extract, and orange zest until blended.

■ Heat a 10″ x 18″ non-stick double-burner pan over medium heat. Brush half the oil over the pan. Using a ¼-cup measure, spoon 10 pancakes into the pan. Cook until the bottoms of the pancakes are set, about 2 minutes. Carefully turn the pancakes over and cook until cooked through, about 1 minute longer.

■ Repeat with the remaining tablespoon of oil and batter. Sprinkle the remaining 3 tablespoons sugar over the pancakes and serve with maple syrup, if you like.

Serves 4

Ingredients

1	(15-ounce) container whole-milk ricotta
6	tablespoons all-purpose flour
4	tablespoons sugar
2	large eggs
1	tablespoon butter, melted and cooled
1	teaspoon vanilla extract
½	teaspoon freshly grated orange zest
2	tablespoons vegetable oil
	Maple syrup, optional

Pumpkin Risotto

If pumpkins or butternut squash are in season, cook one and use it instead of the canned. Look for pumpkin puree, not pumpkin pie mix. Cooked in a non-stick pan, the risotto doesn't stick and is deliciously creamy.

DIRECTIONS

■ In a 2-quart non-stick saucepan, melt 1 tablespoon of the butter over low heat. Add the onion and cook, stirring frequently, until tender, about 7 minutes. Add the rice and stir until well coated. Add the wine and cook, stirring once or twice, until the wine has been absorbed.

■ Meanwhile, combine the broth, sage, salt, pepper, and saffron threads in a 2-quart saucepan and heat over low heat. Add ½ cup of the warm broth mixture to the rice and cook, stirring frequently, until the broth has been absorbed. Continue adding broth, ½ cup at a time, and stirring until the rice is creamy.

■ Stir in the pumpkin and sugar and cook until heated through. Stir in the Parmesan and the remaining tablespoon of butter until well combined. Serve with additional pepper and Parmesan, if you like.

Serves 4

Ingredients

2	tablespoons unsalted butter
1	medium onion, finely chopped (¾ cup)
1¼	cups Arborio rice
¾	cup dry white wine
3¾	cups chicken broth
1	teaspoon dried sage, crumbled
¾	teaspoon salt
½	teaspoon freshly ground black pepper
	Pinch of saffron threads
2	cups solid-pack pumpkin puree (not pumpkin pie mix)
2	teaspoons sugar
½	cup freshly grated Parmesan cheese

Jerry Stiller & Anne Meara

Jerry Stiller and Anne Meara have worked steadily in show business since the landmark appearances they made on the 1950s *Ed Sullivan Show* as an acclaimed stand-up comedy team. They went on to individual careers, but continued to work together when fate and showbiz opportunity came knocking.

Jerry is best known for his role on *Seinfeld* as Frank Costanza–George Costanza's father. After a quarter century of doing Shakespeare, Mamet, Ibsen, and Shaw, Jerry found himself one of America's most famous and beloved actors because of a sitcom. Anne also made a name for herself in television, with roles in *Kate McShane*, *Archie Bunker's Place*, *Alf*, and *Rhoda*. Most recently, she won major kudos as a playwright for her highly regarded play *After Play*.

Potato Pancakes with Smoked Salmon and Chives

Ingredients

2	large Idaho potatoes (1½ pounds), peeled and shredded
1	parsnip (4 ounces), peeled and shredded
3	scallions, thinly sliced
¾	teaspoon salt
½	teaspoon freshly ground black pepper
3	tablespoons olive oil
¼	cup sour cream
2	teaspoons snipped fresh chives
½	teaspoon freshly grated lemon zest
3	slices smoked salmon, quartered crosswise

Potato pancakes usually soak up a lot of oil, but not these—they're crisp and light, thanks to a non-stick skillet.

DIRECTIONS

■ In a medium bowl, stir together the potatoes, parsnip, scallions, salt, and pepper until well combined.

■ Preheat the oven to 400°F. In a 12-inch skillet, heat 1 tablespoon of the oil over medium heat until hot but not smoking. Drop the potato mixture by well-rounded tablespoonfuls into the prepared pan, cooking 6 pancakes at a time, and cook until golden brown, about 3 minutes per side. Transfer to a baking sheet. Repeat, adding oil as needed, until all the pancakes have been browned. (You should have 24 pancakes.) Then, bake the pancakes until they are cooked through, about 5 minutes.

■ Meanwhile, in a small bowl, stir together the sour cream, chives, and lemon zest. Transfer the potato pancakes to a large platter. Top each pancake with a slice of salmon and a dollop of sour cream.

Serves 4 to 6

Jerry Stiller & Anne Meara

Meatballs and Spaghetti

The combination of beef and pork produces a very light, tender meatball.

DIRECTIONS

■ In an 8-inch skillet, heat 2 teaspoons of the olive oil over low heat. Add the onion and garlic and cook, stirring frequently, until the onion is tender, about 7 minutes.

■ In a large bowl, with a fork, combine the bread and milk until pasty. Add the pork, beef, egg, Parmesan cheese, salt, oregano, pepper, and onion mixture; gently mix together. Shape into 24 large meatballs.

■ Dredge the meatballs in the flour, shaking off the excess. In a 5-quart sauté pan, heat the remaining oil over medium heat. Sauté the meatballs until golden brown, about 5 minutes. Add the tomatoes and their juice and bring to a boil. Reduce the heat, cover, and simmer until the meatballs are cooked through, about 15 minutes.

■ Meanwhile, in an 8-quart stockpot of boiling salted water, cook the spaghetti until "al dente"; drain. Transfer to a large bowl with the meatballs and sauce, and toss to combine. Serve with additional Parmesan, if you like.

Serves 4

Ingredients

2	tablespoons olive oil
1	medium onion, finely chopped
2	cloves garlic, minced
1	(1-ounce) slice firm, white, sandwich bread, finely crumbed
1/4	cup milk
6	ounces ground pork
6	ounces ground beef
1	large egg
1/3	cup freshly grated Parmesan cheese
3/4	teaspoon salt
3/4	teaspoon dried oregano, crumbled
1/2	teaspoon freshly ground black pepper
1/4	cup all-purpose flour
2 1/2	cups canned tomatoes, chopped or crushed, with their juice
12	ounces spaghetti

Martin Yan

Chef Martin Yan, celebrated cooking show host, respected food and restaurant consultant, and certified master chef, enjoys distinction as both teacher and author. His many talents have found unique expression in twenty best-selling cookbooks, including his recent, *Martin Yan's Feast: The Best of Yan Can Cook*.

Born in China and professionally trained in Hong Kong, Chef Yan has loved cooking from an early age. He was the first Asian chef to host a half-hour Chinese cooking program, and has been the host of the immensely popular *Yan Can Cook* show on PBS for two decades. Watched and enjoyed by billions of fans worldwide, his shows are as entertaining as they are educational. The *Yan Can Cook* show has won numerous acknowledgements such as a 1998 Daytime Emmy Award, several awards and nominations from the James Beard Foundation, and Finalist for the 1999 World Food Media Award in Australia.

Mongolian Beef

DIRECTIONS

■ In a medium bowl, stir together the dark soy sauce, rice wine, and cornstarch. Add the beef and stir to coat. Let stand 10 minutes at room temperature.

■ Place a wok over high heat until hot. Add 2 tablespoons of the oil, swirling to coat the sides of the pan. With a slotted spoon, lift the beef from the marinade and stir-fry until no longer pink, 1½ to 2 minutes. With a slotted spoon, transfer the beef to a bowl.

■ Add the remaining 1½ teaspoons oil to the wok, swirling to coat the sides. Add the garlic and chilies; cook, stirring, until fragrant, about 10 seconds. Add the green onions and stir-fry 1 minute.

■ Return the beef to the wok. Add the hoisin and soy sauce; cook until heated through.

Serves 4

Ingredients

2	tablespoons dark soy sauce
2	tablespoons Chinese rice wine or dry sherry
1	teaspoon cornstarch
³/₄	pound flank steak, thinly sliced
2	tablespoons plus 1½ teaspoons vegetable oil
2	tablespoons minced garlic
10	small dried red chilies
10	green onions, cut into 3-inch pieces
2	tablespoons hoisin sauce
1	tablespoon soy sauce

Golden Shrimp Toast

Ingredients

10   day-old slices white sandwich bread

Shrimp Paste

$1/4$ cup water chestnuts

$1/2$ pound medium raw shrimp, shelled and deveined

1   egg white

2   teaspoons cornstarch

2   teaspoons Chinese rice wine or dry sherry

$1/2$ teaspoon minced peeled fresh ginger

$1/2$ teaspoon salt

$1/8$ teaspoon white pepper

1   green onion, minced

10   medium raw shrimp, shelled and deveined

     Cooking oil for deep-frying

DIRECTIONS

■ With a 2-inch cookie cutter, cut 2 circles from each bread slice; set aside.

■ Place the water chestnuts in a food processor; pulse until coarsely chopped. Add the remaining shrimp paste ingredients except the green onion. Process until the mixture forms a chunky paste. Transfer to a bowl; stir in the green onion.

■ Spread shrimp paste about $1/4$ inch thick on 1 side of each bread circle. Cut whole shrimp in half lengthwise. Curl 1 shrimp half on top of each bread circle, pressing it firmly into the shrimp paste.

■ In a wok, heat the oil for deep-frying to 350°F. Deep-fry the rounds, a few at a time and shrimp side down, 1 minute. Turn over and cook until golden brown, about 1 minute longer. With a slotted spoon, transfer the shrimp toasts to a paper-towel-lined platter to drain. Serve warm.

Makes 20

The ABC's of the Kitchen

By Chef Martin Yan

Cooking definitely has its own language. Whether you're braising meat or using a Dutch oven, sometimes a little translation is helpful in understanding how to prepare a delicious meal.

I've taken the guesswork out of some of the most popular methods and cookware, by providing sort of a dictionary of the common cooking terms, so you're never confused in the kitchen again:

Baste: Spoon or brush food as it cooks with melted butter or other fat, meat drippings, or liquid such as stock.

Blanch: To submerge food briefly in boiling liquid, remove, and plunge into cold water to stop further cooking. Great for making vegetables such as asparagus or broccoli more appealing as an appetizer served with a dipping sauce.

Braise: A two-step process that starts with browning meat in a small amount of oil to seal in juices. Next, food is cooked at a slow simmer with added liquid in a covered pan. The second step may take place on the stovetop, in the oven, or in a slow cooker.

Brown: Cooking quickly over high heat, causing the surface of the food to turn brown while the interior stays moist.

Caramelize: Heating sugar until it liquifies and becomes a clear syrup ranging in color from golden to dark brown.

Deglaze: After sautéing food and removing excess fat from the pan, deglazing is done by heating a small amount of liquid (usually wine or stock) in a pan and stirring to loosen browned bits of food on the bottom.

Poach: To submerge food in a liquid (usually water, stock, or court bouillon) held at a temperature between 160°F and 180°F. The surface of the liquid should show only slight movement, and have no bubbles. To poach food, bring the poaching liquid to a boil then add the food to be poached.

Reduce: To boil down a liquid to make it thicker and intensify its flavor.

Roast: To oven-cook food in an open pan without liquid. A quick, delicious method of preparing tender pieces of meat. For a crusty, brown exterior on roasted vegetables, coat with oil before placing them in the pan. Roasted food should be cooked in a single layer with room for air circulation. An overcrowded pan may cause food to steam rather than roast.

Roux: A mixture of fat and flour cooked slowly over low heat and used as a thickener for sauces, soups, and gravies.

Sauté: To cook food briefly over medium-high heat in a skillet with a small amount of oil or fat. Food should be stirred to ensure even cooking.

Sear: To brown the surface of meat quickly in a hot pan, oven, or under a broiler.

sometimes a little translation is helpful in understanding how to prepare a delicious meal.

Open French skillet: Used for cooking omelets, pancakes, quesadillas, sautéing vegetables, and searing meats, fish, and poultry. The skillet's sloped sides allow food to slide out easily and our non-stick surfaces make clean-up effortless.

Sauté pan: Sauté pans have a long side handle. These are used for sautéing meats and vegetables, frying chicken, or grilling sandwiches. Deep sides provide extra capacity, allowing you to sear meats and add liquid to the pan to braise, stew, or deglaze.

Sauteuse: Sauteuses have two side handles, enabling the pan to fit neatly in the oven as well as to be used on the range top.

Chef's pan: The chef pan's rounded shape allows efficient stirring or sautéing. From sauces to stir-frys, you'll use this pan every day.

Sauciette: A small, open saucepan with a pouring spout that is perfect for heating milk, wine, syrup, melting butter, or for preparing small quantities of sauces.

Saucepan: Used for cooking sauces and grains, reheating liquids, and more. Our pans conduct heat evenly and are ideal for delicate sauces.

Saucepot: Saucepots are ideal for the slow, gentle simmering of soups, stocks, beans, chili, or for the rapid boiling needed for pasta.

Stockpot: Stockpots are ideal for the slow, gentle simmering of soups, stocks, beans, chili, or for the rapid boiling needed for pasta and lobster.

Dutch oven: Ideal for stews or pot roasts that require searing or browning on the range top and are finished in the oven. The metal handles mean the Dutch oven can be used on top of the stove or in the oven up to 500°F.

Steamer: Steaming is a healthy way to prepare vegetables. The steamer insert holds food over boiling water, allowing steam to circulate, cooking your vegetables and reducing the nutrient loss that occurs in boiling. Stock, lemon, or herbs may be added for flavor.

Pasta insert: Stainless-steel, perforated inserts eliminate the need for a colander to drain pasta. Ideal for cooking delicate foods such as ravioli, which are protected when lifted gently out of the water instead of poured.

Double boiler: The double boiler holds foods above boiling water, protecting them from the harsh direct heat of a burner. Used when delicate preparation is called for, such as melting chocolate or preparing hollandaise sauce, cooked frostings, and some custards.

Round grill pan: Raised grates hold meat or vegetables up high, allowing fat to drip down for low-fat grilling and giving food appealing grill marks. The channel around the sides of the pan collects cooked-off fat. Use to grill meats, fish, and vegetables.

Grill pan: See *Round grill pan*.

Stir-fry: Stir-fry pans have a slightly deeper bowl shape and one long handle. Proper stir-fry technique calls for fast rotating or stirring of ingredients.

Wok: Woks have either two side handles or a long side and helper handle and are wider in diameter. They also have rounded, sloped sides. The shape is similar to that of a salad bowl, which allows for easy tossing of foods.

Round griddle: The low sides of griddles allow maximum access to the cooking surface of the pan and are ideal for breakfast foods like pancakes, eggs, and French toast as well as grilled sandwiches or quesadillas.

Square griddle: See *Round griddle*.

Double-burner griddle: See *Round griddle*.

Rectangular roaster: Metal-handled roasters feature handles that can be used on top of the stove or in the oven up to 500°F, allowing you to brown a roast on the stovetop and finish it in the oven or to roast a turkey in the oven and then transfer it to the stove top.

Oval roaster: Features a stainless-steel lid. See *Rectangular roaster*.

Fiction & Facts

Thinking about investing in non-stick cookware but you're afraid that it's going to be more work than it's worth? Or, perhaps you've heard that non-sticks scratch very easily and once scratched, your cookware is yesterday's news?

Here's the fiction and the facts about non-stick coated cookware from DuPont Autograph®.

Fiction: There are lots of do's and don'ts associated with non-stick pans. They require a lot of extra care and attention.

Fact: Not true. Non-sticks are specifically designed to save time and trouble in the kitchen. Cooking and cleaning is actually easier with non-stick pans. You can simply wash with hot, soapy water after each use.

Fiction: Non-sticks should never go into the dishwasher.

Fact: Dishwasher cleaning is perfectly safe for all DuPont non-sticks. However, you should always read the manufacturer's care instructions to make sure the pan itself is dishwasher safe.

Fiction: You can't store food in the refrigerator in a non-stick pan.

Fact: Yes, you can, with no problems whatsoever.

Fiction: Serious cooks or chefs do not use non-sticks.

Fact: Major advancements in non-stick technology over the past ten years have elevated non-sticks to the performance calibre required by serious cooks and professional chefs. You'll find DuPont non-sticks on professional-quality pans, including stainless steel and hard-anodized aluminum. Premium non-sticks such as DuPont Autograph® are tailored specifically for the cookware they have been applied to and are durable enough to withstand intense use.

Fiction: Non-sticks don't work well for searing foods.

Fact: Searing is easily accomplished in a non-stick pan. Simply preheat your non-stick pan slowly until it reaches the appropriate temperature, then add the food to be seared.

Fiction: One scratch and a non-stick pan is ruined for good.

Fact: With today's improved non-sticks, scratching is much less of a problem to worry about. And even if a minor scratch were to occur, it only affects the appearance –not the cooking or easy clean-up performance–of the pan. To avoid scratching, don't use sharp-edged or metal utensils when cooking. Non-stick coatings like Autograph® resist damage from most metal utensils.

Non-stick pans with **textured bottoms** should be treated like any other non-stick pan, and will provide many years of great performance and easy clean-up.

Fiction: Some cooking techniques, like deglazing, just don't work in a non-stick pan.

Fact: Gourmet cookware with Autograph® is now available and features textured bottoms with super-durable non-sticks. These pans have either pockets or grooves that hold food residue created by the browning process, which can then be used to deglaze. This is a perfect example of how non-sticks are meeting the needs of even today's most serious cooks.

Fiction: If a pan has a textured bottom, food can get stuck in the pattern.

Fact: A DuPont non-stick eliminates the problem of sticking. The superior food release is in no way diminished by these textured surfaces. In fact, these pans can actually extend the performance of a non-stick coating by minimizing the contact between the surface and utensils. Non-stick pans with textured bottoms should be treated like any other non-stick pan, and will provide many years of great performance and easy clean-up.

Fiction: High heat will damage the pan's non-stick finish.

Fact: Low to medium-high heat is recommended for cookware with non-stick surfaces but, on occasion, when it is necessary to cook with temperatures up to 500°F, you can do so without damaging the finish.

Fiction: Is there any guarantee that particles of non-stick coating won't come off during cooking and get into the food?

Fact: With over thirty years experience in non-stick technology, DuPont knows how to ensure that their non-sticks stay on the pan. Extremely durable, DuPont non-sticks are engineered to resist chipping, peeling, flaking, or other kinds of abrasions. What's more, the non-stick coatings themselves are non-toxic, so even if a particle were to be accidentally eaten, it would not be harmful.

A Guide to Gourmet Cookware

Quality cookware is essential to any well-equipped kitchen. Serious cooks who want gourmet results should look for Autograph®, DuPont's most advanced, durable, non-stick on the following lines of cookware:

*A*NOLON
Nouvelle

CIRCULON
PROFESSIONAL

ANODIZED NONSTICK
*A*NOLON

117

Index

Dinner Menu

Accompaniments

Beverage

Dinner Menu

Accompaniments

Beverage

Dinner Menu

Accompaniments

Beverage

Lunch Menu

Accompaniments

Beverage

Lunch Menu

Accompaniments

Beverage